The Green Grass Grows All Around

retold by Ruby Mae
illustrated by Stacey Schuett

HARCOURT BRACE & COMPANY

Orlando Atlanta Austin Boston San Francisco Chicago Dallas New York
Toronto London

In my backyard there is some ground,
The nicest ground you ever did see.
And the green grass grows
all around, all around,
And the green grass grows all around.

And in that ground there is a tree,
The finest tree you ever did see.
Tree in the ground
And the green grass grows
all around, all around,
And the green grass grows all around.

And on that tree there is a nest,
The safest nest you ever did see.
Nest in the tree in the ground
And the green grass grows
all around, all around,
And the green grass grows all around.

And in that nest there is a bird,
The prettiest bird you ever did see.
Bird in the nest in the tree in the ground
And the green grass grows
all around, all around,
And the green grass grows all around.